OPERATION

DESERT STORM

Essential Events

OPERATION

DESERT STORM

BY MARTIN GITLIN

Content Consultant
Chad Lares
President of the Museum of Military History
Independence High School
Loudoun County Public Schools

ABDO
Publishing Company

CREDITS

Published by ABDO Publishing Company, 8000 West 78th Street, Edina, Minnesota 55439. Copyright © 2009 by Abdo Consulting Group, Inc. International copyrights reserved in all countries. No part of this book may be reproduced in any form without written permission from the publisher. The Essential Library™ is a trademark and logo of ABDO Publishing Company.

Printed in the United States.

Editor: Paula Lewis
Copy Editor: Amy Van Zee
Interior Design and Production: Ryan Haugen and Emily Love
Cover Design: Emily Love

Library of Congress Cataloging-in-Publication Data
Gitlin, Marty
  Operation desert storm / By Martin Gitlin.
     p. cm.
  Includes bibliographical references and index.
  ISBN 978-1-60453-516-7
  1. Persian Gulf War, 1991—Juvenile literature. I. Title.

DS79.723.G58 2009
956.704'3—dc22

2008033102

TABLE OF CONTENTS

Tomahawk cruise missiles were fired from the USS Wisconsin.

FIRE FROM THE SKY

At 7:00 p.m. eastern standard time (EST) on January 16, 1991, darkness descended upon most of the United States. Typically, people would be relaxing after a hard day's work. But this day was different—61 million people across the nation anxiously watched television. The attack on Iraq was about to begin.

Suddenly, televised images showed flashes of light over the Iraqi capital of Baghdad. The skies were lit up by antiaircraft fire. Bombs exploded throughout the city. The frightened people of Iraq experienced the horrors of war. The bombs fell in response to Iraq's invasion and takeover of Kuwait five months earlier. Iraq's dictator, Saddam Hussein, had refused to withdraw his troops from the small, helpless nation.

Hussein had ignored his opportunities to withdraw. On several occasions, the United Nations (UN) demanded that he pull his military forces out of Kuwait. The demands were ignored. The final deadline of January 15, 1991, came and went. There would be no more talk. It was time for action.

The initial terror from the skies came from Hellfire missiles and 70-millimeter rockets fired from Apache helicopters. Their goal

Speaking Out

The pro-Iraqi newspaper *al-Rai* was based in the neighboring country of Jordan. As war approached, a headline in the newspaper provided the opposite sentiment of most of the world. "We fight with the sword of God. The U.S. fights with the sword of Satan," it read.[1] The leaders of a few other Arab and African nations spoke out against the efforts of the United States.

was to knock out Iraqi radar detection. Mission accomplished.

The next U.S. missiles were launched from F-117A stealth fighter-bombers. The Iraqis sent antiaircraft artillery skyward. The sky was lit up similar to a massive fireworks display with bursts of orange and red. Guided by lasers, the missiles destroyed Iraqi military command and control centers.

Explosions blasted all around veteran stealth pilot Major Greg Feest. The Iraqis could not aim at specific fighters, but one lucky shot on the Iraqis' part could end his life. And he knew it. "I was praying that I would make it through, but I had to go through it to get to my next target," Feest explained after the war. "I was surprised when I did."[2]

Remarkably, all but one U.S. fighter pilot remained safe as Iraqi antiaircraft continued to blast away. The Iraqis were not as fortunate. With only 25 Iraqi planes airborne, 8 were shot down. U.S. Air Force Captain Steve Tate shot down an Iraqi plane with a Sparrow missile. Tate later stated,

Everywhere, the cities were lighted. And then you saw a twinkling begin, like Christmas lights, in all colors. It was

the triple-A [antiaircraft artillery] being shot at us and the other aircraft. . . . The solid streams of tracers from the [Iraqi guns] looked like colored snakes streaking up. The real heavy artillery would blink on the ground, then explode like big popcorn puffs at 30,000 feet—our altitude.[3]

The Tomahawk Land Attack Missiles (TLAMs) began to arrive with their destructive force of 1,000-pound (454-kg) explosive warheads. One missile slammed into the main Iraqi communications center, knocking out most radio and television stations in Baghdad. Other TLAMs destroyed power plants in Baeiji, Douri, and Taji.

INTO THE LIVING ROOMS OF U.S. CITIZENS

Cable News Network (CNN) officials had persuaded the Iraqi government to grant them permission to hook up a special phone line with a satellite connection that allowed for a broadcast.

CNN newscasters Peter Arnett and John Holliman worked from a ninth-floor room of the Al-Rashid

Other Nations Agree

Before attacking Iraq, President George H. W. Bush spent much of his time speaking with world leaders such as Mikhail Gorbachev of the Soviet Union. Bush wanted a consensus of their feelings. Only after discussions with those leaders, as well as dozens of U.S. political officials and personal friends, did he conclude that war was justified.

Hotel in Baghdad. Soon they were reporting back to the United States. They placed microphones outside their hotel windows so viewers could hear antiaircraft bursts to supplement the sight of flashes in the sky. Sirens screamed. The video communication was broken moments later, but Arnett and Holliman continued to supply information.

At 6:38 p.m. EST, White House Press Secretary Marlin Fitzwater officially announced,

The liberation of Kuwait has begun. In conjunction with the forces of our coalition partners, the United States has moved,

Fateful Decision

Only 13 hours remained until midnight, marking the extended deadline for Iraqi leader Saddam Hussein to pull his troops out of Kuwait. U.S. President George H. W. Bush assembled his closest aides.

Bush had given Hussein the rest of the day to withdraw from Kuwait. By midnight on January 16, war had become a certainty. Bush signed the historic order to attack Iraq.

In his address to the nation, Bush stated,

Our objectives are clear: Saddam Hussein's forces will leave Kuwait. The legitimate government of Kuwait will be restored to its rightful place, and Kuwait will once again be free. Iraq will eventually comply with all relevant United Nations resolutions, and then, when peace is restored, it is our hope that Iraq will live as a peaceful and cooperative member of the family of nations, thus enhancing the security and stability of the Gulf.[4]

Although Bush, like many U.S. citizens, had doubts at times about the morality of going to war, he shed all those doubts by mid-January. He remained confident that he had made the right decision throughout the Gulf War.

under the code name Operation Desert Storm, to enforce the mandates of the United Nations Security Council.[5]

At 9:00 p.m. EST, U.S. President George H. W. Bush addressed the nation. He spoke about Saddam Hussein's defiance of the UN's demand that Iraq pull out of Kuwait. The president also explained his belief that U.S. military action would set a tone for the future.

WORLDWIDE EFFORT

Although the great majority of the forces were from the United States, the U.S. military did not act alone that evening. Coalition partners included Saudi Arabia as well as traditional allies such as Great Britain, France, and Canada. Iraqi airfields were targeted by British warplanes. Fighter jets from Saudi Arabia, France, and Italy participated in the bombing of Iraqi missile launch sites. Combat troops from around the world waited to begin their ground assault as Baghdad was bombed.

The strategic bombing severely crippled Iraqi defenses. The Tomahawks, which were fired from nine ships, sent missiles into the heart of Baghdad. Most were aimed at military and communication

Darkness

By the time the Tomahawk Land Attack Missiles had landed in Iraq on the first night of bombings, pilots reported that the only light in Baghdad was created by explosions in the sky. The city had descended into darkness as many of the buildings or their lighting systems had been destroyed.

centers. Thirty missiles struck the sprawling missile complex at Taji. But other attacks shook the nerve center of Iraqi political officials. Eight missiles exploded into the presidential palace. Six more hit the Baath Party headquarters.

Iraqis were stunned. They had been told by Hussein that they would win the battle against the United States. The night of terror destroyed strategic sites in the city, and it destroyed the optimism of the people of Baghdad. As dawn approached, the last U.S. fighter planes left the area. The Iraqi screams of defiance against the invaders had turned into cries of despair.

That despair had just begun for Saddam Hussein and the Iraqi people. But how did they incur the anger of the world? Insight into the recent history of Hussein's country and his barbaric rule tell that story. ✐

*President George H. W. Bush in the Oval Office on January 17, 1991,
as efforts were made to force Iraqis out of Kuwait.*

On January 17, 1991, Defense Secretary Dick Cheney (left) and General
Colin Powell (right) announced the loss of a U.S. plane in the attack on Iraq.

SEEDS OF DISCONTENT

On January 17, 1991, Operations Order
91-001 was sent from U.S. Defense
Secretary Richard (Dick) Cheney to General
Norman Schwarzkopf. The United States understood
the importance of isolating and incapacitating

the Iraqis. The order clearly stated the objective of the attack on Iraq:

> Attack Iraqi political-military leadership and command and control; gain and maintain air superiority; sever Iraqi supply lines; destroy known chemical, biological and nuclear production, storage, and delivery facilities; destroy [Iraqi forces in Kuwait]; and liberate Kuwait City.[1]

The relationship between the United States and Iraq had reached a dangerous state.

MESOPOTAMIA

The history of Iraq, once known as Mesopotamia, goes back to biblical times. The United States became interested in Mesopotamia in 1908. Oil was discovered that year in the neighboring country of Persia (now Iran). With the awareness that oil was abundant throughout the Middle East, industrialized nations of the world took notice. The need for oil grew with the outbreak of World War I in 1914. Great Britain in particular sought oil for its tanks and warships.

Independence

The official granting of independence to the nation of Iraq did not occur until 1927. Great Britain installed Emir Faisal as king of the newly proclaimed Kingdom of Iraq in 1921. However, Great Britain did not declare Iraq to be a free and independent nation until six years later.

Much of the Middle East had been under the colonial control of Great Britain for more than a century. When Turkish troops fought on the side of the Germans, Great Britain dispatched troops into the Mesopotamian area of Basra and gained control. Although they had promised independence to Mesopotamia, an agreement with France after the war divided up the entire Middle East between both countries. Independence, however, was soon granted.

THE FAITH FACTOR

For centuries, religion has played a critical role in the affairs of Iraq and the entire Middle East. The Muslim faith has been dominant in Iraq since the prophet Mohammed founded the religion of Islam in the seventh century.

After the death of Mohammed, a disagreement over religious leadership led to the division of Muslims into Sunnis and Shiites. These branches are still at odds. Approximately 85 percent of Muslims are Sunnis. Egypt and Saudi Arabia have Sunni majorities. Iran is the only nation with an overwhelming majority of Shiites. Iraq and Lebanon have some large Shiite areas.

The deep and unbending belief in particular religious ideas resulted in a people who are often motivated more by their faith than by their nationality. Many Iraqis, and Muslims from other nations, became so strongly religious that they veered away from the peaceful teachings of Mohammed and developed intolerance for other faiths. The preference of religion over patriotism in Iraq was an issue that future leader Saddam Hussein would attempt to change.

OIL

The United States became particularly interested in the region during World War II (1939–1945). In an attempt to help the Soviet Union repel the Germans, the United States established the Persian Gulf Command in Iran and sent approximately 4 million tons (3.6 million tonnes) of supplies to the Soviet Union.

By that time, it had become apparent that the U.S. economy would soon become very dependent on oil from that area of the world.

Standard Oil

The first U.S. link to oil in the Middle East was established in 1933. Standard Oil of California agreed to begin purchasing oil from Saudi Arabia for consumption in the United States. The Middle East became vitally important to the U.S. economy at that time and remains so to this day.

In 1947, U.S. Secretary of the Navy James Forrestal stated,

> *. . . Middle East oil [is] going to be necessary for this country not merely in wartime but in peacetime . . . if we are going to make the contribution that it seems we have to make to the rest of the world in manufactured goods, we shall probably need very greatly increased supplies of fuel.* [2]

A New Arab World

Many Middle Eastern nations emerged from World War II as independent nations; others did not become independent until 1971. The League of Arab States was quickly formed to speak for the interests of its countries. But this was not a peaceful time. Jewish settlers who had survived the mass murder of their people by German dictator Adolf Hitler began pouring into their ancient homeland of Palestine and declared the nation of Israel.

The United Nations recognized Israel as an independent country in 1948, but the Arab nations claimed that the Jewish people had no right to Palestine, which had been occupied by Arabs. Soon Iraq and its Arab neighbors invaded Palestine. Israel not only drove them back, but gained territory.

On January 27, 1969, Saddam Hussein, a leading member of the Baath Party, spoke after 14 Iraqis accused of spying for Israel were sentenced to death by hanging.

The United States has proven to be a strong ally of Israel ever since, a reality that remains a source of constant friction between the United States and most of the Arab world.

A number of factions, or groups, fought for control of Iraq. A military takeover in 1958 established the Republic of Iraq and Abdul Karim Kassem as its leader. The newly formed Baath Party failed in its attempt to murder Kassem a year later. Hussein was among those involved. When the plot failed, Hussein fled to Syria and then to Egypt.

Tension between Iraq and Kuwait began in 1961 when Kuwait gained independence from Great Britain. Kassem declared that Iraq owned Kuwait and ordered troops to its borders. Great Britain sent ground forces to the area and forced Iraq to withdraw.

Saddam Hussein

The Baath Party gained power in Iraq in 1963, and Hussein returned from exile. However, the Baath Party was quickly removed by the military, which claimed that the party had not gained the support of the Iraqi people. The Baath Party regained control in 1968, whereupon Hussein was placed in charge of the nation's internal security. He ran it ruthlessly as thousands of people deemed dangerous to Baath Party dominance were murdered. Within two years, Hussein became the most influential figure in Iraq.

The Arab oil embargo of 1973 nearly quadrupled the cost of oil to the United States and other foreign countries. However, the higher price of oil brought in much-needed money to the Baath Party by adding $80 billion to the Iraq economy over the next seven years. Iraq was becoming a more powerful country.

With the resignation of Ahmed Hassan al-Bakr in 1979, Hussein assumed control of Iraq. He perceived enemies everywhere and ordered one-third of the party leadership shot to death. Initially, Hussein forged friendly ties with the United States. He attempted to establish positive relationships through trade with countries such as the Soviet Union and France. But trouble was brewing in Iran. The shah of Iran (who was backed by the United States) was overthrown in favor of Ayatollah Khomeini, a strict Shiite Muslim

Shocking Gas Prices

The price of gasoline had barely increased during the 1960s and early 1970s. Gas stations competed for customers in price wars by selling gasoline for as little as 19¢ a gallon. But the gas shortage caused by the Arab oil embargo of 1973 resulted in many service stations running out of gas. It also caused a major increase in the price of gas.

As 1973 began, the average cost of a gallon of gas in the United States was about 59¢. By 1981, it had increased to $1.40.

The United States promoted the concept of conserving gas and decreasing demand for it. In many states, gas was rationed. The days a person could purchase gas were dependent on an odd/even system. Owners of vehicles with plates ending with an odd number could buy gas on odd-numbered dates. Owners of vehicles with plates ending with an even number could buy gas on even-numbered dates.

To decrease the demand for oil, the national maximum speed limit was lowered to 55 miles per hour (88.5 km/h). Automakers downsized cars and decreased the weight of cars to increase fuel efficiency. Commuters were encouraged to use more mass transit and to carpool whenever possible.

fundamentalist. He had been expelled from Iraq in 1978.

The following November, Shiite extremists raided the American embassy in the Iranian capital of Tehran and took 66 hostages. They demanded that the shah, who was receiving medical treatment in the United States, be returned to Iran to stand trial for crimes against their nation. The United States refused.

Balance of Power

Hussein was a Sunni Muslim in a largely Shiite Iraq. The United States understood the importance of keeping him in power. If Hussein lost power, Iraq could easily be taken over by Shiites. In turn, this could lead to Iran and Iraq emerging as one united power.

The extremists held the hostages for more than a year. The relationship between the United States and Iran has remained strained.

But it was Iraq that actually provoked a war against Iran. Years earlier, Iran had taken control of an important waterway to the Persian Gulf. Hussein wanted the waterway back and attacked Iran in September 1980. The vicious ruler had started down the road of attempting military solutions to achieve his goals. He never strayed from that path.

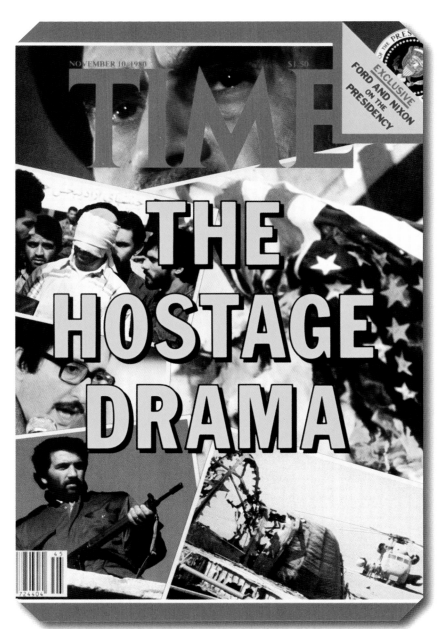

The cover of a November 10, 1980, TIME magazine shows photos of the hostage crisis.

*Iraqi President Saddam Hussein on November 2, 1980,
just days after sending troops into Iran*

COLLISION COURSE

hen Saddam Hussein sent Iraqi tanks
and troops into Iran on September
22, 1980, it did not immediately signal war against
the United States. But it did show that Hussein
would take a military approach to disagreements with

foreign nations, which he also displayed a decade later in his invasion of Kuwait. Whether or not Hussein had a legitimate complaint against Iran is an issue of debate.

The conflict was based on several factors that included Iran's control of the Shatt al-Arab waterway. But Hussein and Khomeini also had other differences. Hussein based his rule on ruthlessly developing Iraqi patriotism. Khomeini was far more driven by his view of religious principles.

Khomeini began providing support for Iraqi Shiite groups that wanted their government to be run based on strict religious guidelines. Revealing his desire to complete that job, he stated, "What we have done in Iran we will do again in Iraq."[1]

By 1980, Iraq owned the resources to successfully wage war. Oil profits were bringing in $23 billion a year. Much of the money funded the military. Hussein's goal was for Iraq to shed its dependence on other countries. He wanted Iraq to be a world power, but he felt threatened

Oil Profits

The profits gained by the Iraqis from the sale of oil during the 1970s were also used for items other than military equipment. Some of the income was used to provide free education and health care to the Iraqi people and increased salaries for workers. Iraq became one of the more modern Middle Eastern nations during the 1970s despite Hussein's brutality and warlike intentions.

by Iran. Khomeini had already given his support to a radical Shiite group that planned to turn Iraq into an Iranian puppet state.

A desire to dominate the Middle East may have been the major consideration in Hussein's decision to invade Iran in 1980. He wanted to overtake Iran only a year after Khomeini had taken power. King Fahd of Saudi Arabia reported that Hussein admitted, "It is more useful to hit them [the Iranians] now because they are weak. If we leave them until they become strong, they will overrun us."[2]

The invasion began well for Iraq. Hussein's forces seized the disputed

---

Putting on a Show

Saddam Hussein was not a master of propaganda. His barbaric reputation did not allow him to fool many people. But he did his best to put on a friendly face in a film he used during the conflict against Iran. Hussein was shown speaking sweetly to the Iranian children Khomeini had used as soldiers and who had been captured as prisoners of war.

The children sat on comfortable chairs and were dressed in nice shirts and pants. He asked the children if they preferred living in the city or the country. He asked about their families. He asked whether they were students or workers. Then he gathered them around for a group photograph.

"We hope that you can go back to your families and that some of you will become lawyers and engineers," Hussein said to them kindly. "When you pass your exams, let us know, and when the war ends, come back and enjoy our country's hospitality."[3]

The film was presented to foreign visitors to point out that Iran was putting children in harm's way by using them as soldiers.

Shatt al-Arab waterway and occupied a 30-mile (48-km) strip of Iranian territory by the second day. Many world leaders harbored anti-Khomeini sentiment for his support of those who still held U.S. citizens hostage, so they supported Iraq in the battle. But the Iraqis' poor command and the Iranians' strong fighting spirit stalled Iraq's surge.

With his troops bogged down in Iran, Hussein began training an elite unit known as the Republican Guard to protect his country against a possible Iranian counterattack. The Republican Guard had been in existence for decades, but this was the first time it was trained to fight in war conditions. Hussein enticed young men with special privileges to join the elite force.

The war that Hussein hoped would destroy Khomeini served to solidify Khomeini's support among the Iranian people and religious Iraqi Shiites. Khomeini turned to these

Sympathetic Weapons

Khomeini's refusal to end the war in 1982 brought sympathy to Iraq from many nations. The Soviet Union and France supplied Hussein with weapons that he eventually used. He sent his first Scud missiles into Iran in 1982. He also used Scuds and other weapons sent by foreign countries during the Gulf War.

Ayatollah Khomeini in 1978

people and asked for their support to bring down the
Iraqi leader:

> *If you can kill Saddam before we execute him, stab him in the
> back. . . . Paralyze the economy. Stop paying taxes. This is
> war between Islam and blasphemy.*[4]

The Iran-Iraq conflict continued until
Khomeini finally accepted a cease-fire in August
of 1988, six years after Iraq had stopped its
attacks and had taken a strictly defensive position.

The conflict had accomplished nothing but death and destruction. An estimated 500,000 to 1 million men, women, and children died. As many as 2 million more were wounded. Iraq was not able to secure the waterway that initiated the war.

PROBLEMS FOR IRAQ

The bitter conflict left Iraq militarily strong despite the loss of manpower. Its army had quadrupled in size during the war to nearly a million men. But the nation was in financial ruins. In 1980, Iraq had $35 billion in foreign reserves. But by the end of the war in 1988, Iraq owed approximately $100 billion to other countries. The cost of repairing the damage caused by the war was estimated at twice that much.

Among the financial contributors to Iraq was Kuwait, a tiny but wealthy nation on the Persian Gulf. The Iraqi war debt to Kuwait was $8 billion. Hussein stated that he was not going to pay off the debt. He reasoned that since Kuwait was once part of the province of Basra under the Ottoman

Kuwait

Hussein was not the first Iraqi leader to claim that his country should rightfully have control of Kuwait. Many previous Iraqi heads of state believed that Kuwait should have been part of Iraqi territory since Iraq was granted independence in the 1920s. Hussein was the first to act on that claim.

Empire, it should never have been considered an independent nation.

The military strength and financial weakness Iraq faced after the war against Iran motivated Hussein to attack Kuwait. He was also motivated by Kuwait's refusal to forgive Iraq's war debts and loan Iraq more money for rebuilding his war-ravaged nation. Hussein failed to convince Kuwait and other Arab countries to raise oil prices to fund the recovery.

Hussein contemplated the idea of controlling the Kuwaiti coastline on the Persian Gulf. Iraq has little access to critical waterways. Hussein understood that a takeover of Kuwait would double Iraq's control of the world's oil reserves to 20 percent.

The same result in Saudi Arabia, which many thought to be Hussein's next target, would increase Iraq's control of the world's oil reserves to as much as 40 percent. That would mean a possible domination of the entire Arab world.

Hussein underestimated the world's reaction to the invasion of Kuwait. He certainly had been given no reason to fear the United States, which had shown little interest in his country over the years. Hatred for Iran during the hostage crisis had prompted U.S. leaders to back Iraq early in the Iraq-Iran war. After the hostages were released in 1981, the United States took a neutral stand.

Iraq's relations with the United States improved in the early 1980s. President Ronald Reagan removed Iraq from the list of nations supporting terrorism or threatening the use of surprise attacks. But Hussein's rejection of terrorism was merely a statement to convince other countries to help Iraq during the war.

In 1982, U.S. leaders became concerned that Iran would overrun Iraq and take control of its vast oil reserves. Though the United States would not sell arms to Iraq, it encouraged other nations to do so and to help finance the Iraqi war effort. Yet Iraqi foreign minister Tariq Aziz remained skeptical about the intentions of the United States. He believed the United States was thinking more about its own interests. Aziz asked,

> *Do you think we Iraqis have suddenly become the beloved of the Americans? I don't. If Iraq lost the war, the whole area would be brought to chaos and destruction.*[5]

Aziz was right that the United States could never ally itself with Hussein, who had become well known as a vicious dictator. During the war, Hussein

Brutal Dictatorships

Not all world leaders took sides in the war between Iran and Iraq. Some believed that since Khomeini and Hussein were ruthless dictators, both should lose power as a result of the war. U.S. Secretary of State Henry Kissinger was among those who regarded Iran and Iraq as brutal dictatorships and was not against the weakening of both nations.

attacked Iranian invaders and his own Kurdish population with chemical weapons such as mustard gas. This gas burns the skin and lungs and often causes a slow, painful death.

It has been said that the enemy of an enemy is a friend. And during that period, the United States had friendlier relations with Iraq than with Iran. However, this would not last for long.

*U.S. General H. Norman Schwarzkopf, Commander
of the Gulf War allied forces*

On August 6, 1990, the UN Security Council voted in favor of military actions against Iraq for invading Kuwait.

KILLING IN KUWAIT

Saddam Hussein assumed there would be little outcry from the world if he attacked Kuwait. And the Kuwaiti emir assumed Hussein could be pacified by money. The assumptions of both men were wrong.

In February 1990, Hussein asked his Arab neighbors if they could suspend his wartime financial debt to them. His pleas were ignored.

In May, an Arab Summit was held in Baghdad. Its purpose was to discuss the dispute between Kuwait and Iraq over oil resources. This did not result in a peaceful solution.

On July 17, Hussein claimed that Kuwait had hurt Iraq by exceeding oil production limits set by the Organization of Petroleum Exporting Countries (OPEC). By exceeding these limits, Kuwait had driven down the price of oil. Hussein threatened war and sent approximately 30,000 troops, many of them from the elite Republican Guard, to the Kuwaiti border.

The following day, Hussein claimed Kuwait was about to invite the United States and its allies from Western Europe to join in talks about the oil dispute. Hussein wanted the issue decided only by an agreement of Arab nations, and he discussed that possibility with other Arab leaders.

Hussein told Egyptian President Hosni Mubarak that he had no intention of attacking Kuwait while talks were taking place. But only three days later, Hussein ordered an additional 30,000 troops

and 3,000 military vehicles to
the Kuwaiti border. By July 26,
approximately 100,000 Iraqi troops
were ready to strike.

Near the end of July, Kuwaiti
military leaders put their forces on
full alert and placed them north
of Kuwait City, the capital of the
small country. But Emir Sheikh
Jaber al-Ahmed al-Sabah believed
that Hussein was only threatening
war to extract money from Kuwait.
The prospect of talks to resolve the
oil issue motivated the emir to decide that war was
unlikely. He withdrew the troops.

Even the U.S. State Department did not
anticipate an attack. They believed Hussein's
threats were made to provide him an advantage over
Kuwait regarding the price of oil. Another wrong
assumption.

At 1:00 a.m., Iraqi local time, on August 2,
1990, a force of more than 100,000 Iraqi soldiers
and an estimated 2,000 tanks invaded Kuwait. The
Kuwaitis were taken by surprise and unprepared.
The Iraqis drove toward Kuwait City with little

resistance. Helicopters dropped more Iraqi troops at a dozen strategic sites.

Within 12 hours, most of the resistance had been broken and Kuwaiti leaders fled the capital. The emir, as well as Kuwaiti Crown Prince Sa'd Abdullah al-Sabah and the rest of the royal family, fled to Saudi Arabia. Hussein quickly proclaimed Kuwait an Iraqi province.

The invading Iraqis seized a Kuwaiti radio and television station. "O Arabs, Kuwait's blood and honor are being violated," pleaded a voice believed to be the crown prince and picked up on a hidden transmitter. "Rush to its rescue! The children, the women, the old men of Kuwait are calling on you."[1]

Showing No Fear

Most foreign embassies in Kuwait closed after the Iraqi invasion. However, the leaders of the United States, the Soviet Union, Great Britain, and France did not want to appear to be intimidated by Hussein; their embassies remained open.

It was risky, particularly after Hussein took foreign workers hostage. U.S. General Norman Schwarzkopf believed this alone was cause for war. Schwarzkopf was particularly concerned that Hussein would order the execution of the foreign workers.

U.S. leaders recognized that the hostages were in grave danger and considered their options. These included immediate military action. A decision was made to wait until all UN forces were ready to strike.

The release of the foreign hostages in Kuwait in December came as an enormous relief. However, that gesture was not nearly enough to save Hussein from an attack on his country the following month.

BRUTAL TAKEOVER

The invasion was considered aggression. The Iraqi occupiers were brutal. Murder, torture, and rape were common. Torture centers were later discovered. Meat hooks, electric cattle prods, and other instruments to inflict pain were found.

Thousands of innocent Kuwaitis were killed. Some were beaten and murdered for raising the Kuwaiti flag or refusing to replace pictures of the emir with those of Hussein. Iraqi soldiers looted museums. "They tried to wipe out the identity of Kuwait, as if Kuwait did not exist," protested one Kuwaiti citizen.[2]

The barbaric acts were well underway as world leaders contemplated how to respond. Upon learning of the invasion, President George H. W. Bush asked the United Nations (UN) Security Council to call for an immediate withdrawal of all Iraqi troops from Kuwait. The vote to do so was unanimous. Even Arab League countries agreed to military action against Iraq and joined in the effort.

Hussein claimed that his military had simply answered a plea for help from Kuwaitis who had toppled the government. He then sent 150,000 additional soldiers into Kuwait after all resistance was quelled. He ordered thousands of foreigners, including U.S. and British citizens, to be held at military outposts as "human shields" against invaders. And he threatened all who considered a military response. "[Iraq will] make Kuwait a graveyard for those who launch any aggression," warned the dictator.[3]

While his troops tortured and murdered innocent Kuwaitis, Hussein considered himself to be in a position of strength. He offered to discuss a possible peace plan on August 12. He attempted to tie his takeover of Kuwait to other issues in the Middle East, such as Israeli-held territory. But world leaders remained steadfast and insisted that he withdraw from Kuwait.

To gain favor with other Arab countries, Hussein offered to initiate a peace plan that he believed favored them. While anti-American demonstrations were held in Jordan, Yemen, and Lebanon, no Arab countries came to Hussein's aid.

A Tactical Move

One enemy Hussein believed he could win over was Iran. Two weeks after Iraq invaded Kuwait, Hussein offered to establish the middle of the Shatt al-Arab waterway as the border between the two countries, exchange prisoners immediately, and remove all ground troops from Iran. His reasons for making the offer were purely tactical. Hussein eventually moved many of the troops taken out of Iran to the Saudi border.

MAKING A DECISION

Soon after the invasion of Kuwait, U.S. Defense Secretary Dick Cheney and Joint Chiefs of Staff Chairman General Colin Powell discussed an appropriate reply from the United States. Cheney believed that President Bush could not base his actions on public opinion in the United States. He also asked if the objective should be forcing the Iraqis out of Kuwait or extending the fight all the way to Iraq to topple Hussein's regime.

Powell contemplated what the first step would be. He did not want to lose lives over the price of oil. Powell wanted to respond with economic pressure, not with the lives of U.S. military personnel.

Powell's concerns about Saudi Arabia were legitimate. With Iraqi troops already gathered on the Saudi border, there was speculation that Hussein was not going to stop with Kuwait. Saudi King Fahd bin Abdul Aziz al-Saud met with Cheney and General Norman Schwarzkopf to ask for help. The Saudi king's country had a military force of only 65,000 men. They would not be a match for the Iraqis.

Ships soon began to arrive in the Persian Gulf to reinforce a blockade of material coming in and out of Iraq and Kuwait as ordered by the UN.

U.S. Secretary of State James Baker visited troops in the Saudi desert on November 4, 1990. The troops were preparing for military action if Iraq did not withdraw from Kuwait.

The United States and Great Britain also sent troops and warplanes to the area to support Saudi Arabia. Operation Desert Shield had begun.

Clear Intentions

By September, Bush's intentions were clear. Iraq could not be allowed to get away with its invasion. "Iraq will not be permitted to annex Kuwait," he said in a speech to Congress. "That's not a threat or a boast. That's just the way it's going to be."[4]

In November, Bush announced that 200,000 U.S. troops would be sent to the Middle East to supplement the armed forces already there. By the beginning of 1991, coalition forces of approximately 500,000 soldiers were in Saudi Arabia and on nearby warships. The Iraqis began fortifying their positions along the Saudi border.

Tactical debates continued for months. Striking by air alone would not weaken Iraq enough nor secure the freedom of Kuwait. The attack needed to come from both the ground and the air. An air strike would be used first, as an immediate ground war would be difficult to win and costly in the loss of human life.

Bush believed the United States had no business trying to deal with the various political and religious factions in Iraq. Therefore, the United States would not attempt to eliminate Hussein or occupy Iraq. While Bush received support from other Arab countries in ending Iraq's march into Kuwait, the killing of Hussein would not have brought the

An Unpopular War

The actions by President Bush leading up to the Gulf War led to strong criticism by some U.S. citizens. The United States had scarcely recovered from the unpopular Vietnam War, which ended only 15 years earlier. The Vietnam War resulted in the loss of more than 50,000 U.S. lives.

same backing. The decision was made to destroy Hussein's ability to make war.

Some argued that the interests of the United States did not center on Iraq's unjust invasion of Kuwait, but on oil from the Persian Gulf region that was critical to the U.S. economy. The words "no blood for oil" became a popular sentiment among antiwar protesters.

A WAR ABOUT TO BEGIN

World leaders believed that additional bloodshed could be avoided. But an attempt by Soviet Union leader Mikhail Gorbachev to negotiate a peaceful Iraqi withdrawal from Kuwait failed. Bush tried to schedule talks with Iraqi foreign minister Tariq Aziz in late November, but that too fell through. Although Hussein released all foreign hostages the following month, he refused to remove his troops from Kuwait.

Aziz finally met with U.S. Secretary of State James Baker on January 9, 1991, but their talks proved pointless. Hussein stood firm. According to published reports, Hussein's half brother and advisor, Barzan al-Tikriti, told Hussein that the United States did not want to fight. The Iraqi leader still seemed to be ignorant of U.S. intentions when he spoke publicly at that time.

"We are not of the type that bows to threats, and you will see the trap that America will fall into," Hussein said. "If the Americans are involved in a gulf conflict, you will see how we will make them swim in their own blood."[5]

This was not an empty threat. The Iraqis boasted a human arsenal of 900,000 men. Iraq also owned tanks and ammunition that had been purchased over the years from military powers such as the Soviet Union, China, and France. In addition, Iraq had shown a willingness to use chemical weapons and brutality to achieve its goals.

The world, however, could not allow the attack on Kuwait to go unpunished. Three days after the Aziz-Baker meeting ended in failure, the U.S. Senate approved military action against Iraq by a vote of 250–183. The decision was made. The war Hussein believed would never arrive was about to begin. ⌐

*U.S. Marines prepared for war during an exercise
in the Saudi desert on January 12, 1991.*

In January 1991, U.S. troops gathered in a bunker in Saudi Arabia wearing protective gas masks and chemical suits.

FIRST PHASE OF WAR

ilitary troops waited for months in Saudi Arabia for the signal to attack. But the troops also had the impression that war was imminent. On November 29, 1990, the United Nations (UN) passed Resolution 678 calling for military force against Iraq if its troops were not withdrawn from Kuwait by January 15, 1991. The Iraqi training was intensified.

As war became imminent in the Middle East, U.S. General Norman Schwarzkopf thoughtfully wrote a statement to the U.S. forces. It read:

> *Soldiers, sailors, airmen, and marines . . . This morning at [3:00 a.m.] we launched Operation Desert Storm, an offensive campaign that will enforce United Nations resolutions that Iraq must cease its rape and pillage of its weaker neighbor and withdraw its forces from Kuwait. . . . You have trained hard for this battle and you are ready. During my visits with you, I have seen in your eyes a fire of determination to get this job done and done quickly so that we may return to the shores of our great nation. My confidence in you is total. Our cause is just! Now you must be the thunder and lightning of Desert Storm.[1]*

Waiting

Coalition troops awaiting the ground war were stationed in Saudi Arabia or on ships in the Persian Gulf. They spent a great deal of time training for a mission many hoped would not be necessary. They trained in temperatures that often rose to 115 degrees Fahrenheit (46°C) in the daytime. This was an important reason why the ground troops were not going to attack until February, when the temperatures ranged from 45 degrees to 65 degrees Fahrenheit (7°C to 18°C). Otherwise, heat exhaustion would have been a serious problem for the troops in their chemical protective suits.

Instant Thunder

The thunder and lightning were not going to be bored for long. The Instant Thunder air campaign proved to be a tremendous success. Approximately 155 cruise missiles and 300 F-117 missions in the concentrated air attack destroyed its 45 Baghdad targets. The attacks were so precise that often nearby buildings remained intact. Two U.S. aircraft were downed during the bombing.

The precision of the U.S. fighters intimidated the Iraqi military. Through their communication devices, U.S. pilots could hear Iraqi pilots making excuses such as engine problems to avoid going airborne to confront the U.S. fighters. Even a

Riveting Viewing

In an unsuccessful attempt to lure Israel into the war, Iraqi dictator Saddam Hussein ordered Iraqi Scud missiles sent to Israel on January 18, 1991. The fear that chemical weapons were attached to the missiles was given credence by ABC News reporter Frank Reynolds. He was shown wearing a gas mask as a Scud warhead dropped nearby.

U.S. viewers watched nervously as the broadcast briefly went off the air. Many believed that Reynolds had been a victim of a nerve gas bomb. The transmission returned quickly to a visibly frightened Reynolds. He concluded his report, but his situation brought home the fear that Israelis felt.

Although Scud missiles brought terror into the hearts of Israelis, they did little real damage. Eight missiles were sent to Israel shortly after the initial attack on Iraq. More were to arrive in the coming days, but the Israelis continued to go about their daily business with little fear.

token challenge may have thrown the U.S. bombers off target, but they were not met with Iraqi air resistance.

The domination of the skies continued for weeks as coalition forces led by the United States dropped bombs on Iraqi targets night after night. In one month, the heaviest aerial attack in the history of warfare continued to blow up Iraqi command centers, factories, Baath Party headquarters, power stations, bridges, and every conceivable strategic site. Military equipment and tanks were also destroyed.

Although the bombers struck as accurately as possible, civilian casualties were inevitable. The number of Iraqi deaths rose with each passing day. On February 13, 1991, two U.S. stealth bombers targeted what was believed to be a military command post in southwest Baghdad, but it was a civilian shelter housing 400 men, women, and children. Television coverage that showed Iraqi family members weeping and crying out in anger brought the war home to viewers around the world. One Iraqi man said, "The Americans inflicted more damage on our country in two hours than the Iranians did in eight years."[2] U.S. military leaders later admitted their mistake.

IRAQ'S DEFENSE

The Iraqi strategy of taking a defensive approach to the air war failed miserably. Approximately 76 of the Iraqi aircraft flew to Iran to escape the Western allies. The fighters were never returned. Saddam Hussein had a strategy, but his air force lacked the training and will to carry it out.

The Iraqis also failed to attack Saudi Arabia during the early stages of Operation Instant Thunder. This gave the coalition control of the skies. Not only did they freely attack Baghdad and other areas as the Iraqi defenses proved futile, but the coalition forces did not need to defend the skies.

The Iraqi Air Force was equipped with high-performance fighters, but its strategy centered strictly on the defense of Iraq and Kuwait. Iraq simply could not defend itself.

Hussein hoped to lure Israel into the war, thereby convincing other Arab nations to join his side. Shortly after the initial air attack on his country, Hussein sent Scud missiles toward Israel and Saudi Arabia. The Soviet-made Scuds were considered obsolete, but they were Hussein's most powerful weapons. Scuds sent to Israel were falsely rumored to be carrying chemical weapons.

Iraqi Scud missiles attacked Tel Aviv, Israel, on January 18, 1991, one day after Operation Desert Storm was launched.

On January 23, 1991, General Colin Powell announced that the coalition had achieved air superiority. This signaled the end of the air war. Iraq had launched 40 Scud missiles into Israeli territory. Reports vary, but Israeli casualties included approximately 240 Israelis wounded, 1 person died from a Scud attack, and 4 died from heart attacks caused by the shock of the explosions. The psychological damage proved far greater than the military damage.

Air Force F-117 Stealth fighter-bomber

The Israelis planned to launch a massive strike against Iraq by sending planes over Saudi airspace—a plan that King Fahd quickly forbade. U.S. leaders scrambled to advise Israel against military action that might escalate the war and push other Arab nations on the side of Iraq.

Hussein could do little militarily, so he stepped up his threats. He placed the few coalition prisoners of war in front of television cameras and forced them to condemn the attack on Iraq. He warned that the prisoners would be used as human shields against strategic targets around his country, but his threats were largely ignored.

HUSSEIN'S NEW TACTIC

The Iraqis were beaten in the air. However, there was no hint of a coalition ground invasion yet. This prompted Hussein to order the only Iraqi ground attack of the war on January 29, 1991. He believed that losses of life would turn U.S. sentiment against the war and disrupt coalition plans. Hussein sent troops and tanks over the Saudi border.

The surprise night attack at one U.S. position at Umm Hujul ended in the death of 13 marines. Unfortunately, 11 of the marines were the victims of "friendly fire" from their own men that had been caused by darkness and confusion.

The Iraqis had little success. A column of approximately 80 to 100 tanks overran one Saudi National

Dumping Oil

Hussein was angry and frustrated over the failure to draw the Israelis into the war. This led to an order that accomplished little other than destroying the environment. He ordered the oil drained from five Kuwaiti oil tankers docking in the Persian Gulf. An estimated 7 to 9 million barrels of oil were dumped into the water. It destroyed animal and plant life. Its effect on military operations was minimal.

Guard position and occupied the abandoned town of Khafji, whose 20,000 residents had fled weeks earlier. But two days after launching their attack, 100 Iraqi soldiers were dead and as many as 450 were taken prisoner. The failed offensive forced the Iraqis to retreat over their own border to await the coalition ground attack in their country.

While Hussein hailed the "capture" of the deserted Saudi town as a great victory, it was actually one of Iraq's greatest setbacks. Many of the troops repulsing the attack were from Arab countries with obsolete military equipment. Schwarzkopf felt relief in the knowledge that the skill and training of the Iraqi military was vastly overrated. The U.S. Marines came away from the battle of Khafji firm in that same belief. "Get in the first shot at him and the rest will run away," one young marine said of Iraqi soldiers.[3]

Exaggeration

Hussein had a tendency to exaggerate the success of his military. Shortly after the air war began, he claimed that his forces shot 55 U.S. and coalition warplanes out of the sky. However, the coalition governments reported a combined total of only four downed aircraft.

Although an Iraqi missile struck a helicopter over Kuwait and killed 14 more U.S. soldiers, the offensive was a defeat for Hussein and contributed greatly to his eventual doom. He had hoped to start the ground war, destroy the Saudi Army, and kill enough U.S. troops to turn public opinion in the United States against the war.

Hussein also wanted to take thousands of prisoners from coalition forces to use as human shields and barter against attacks on his tanks. Instead, his troops were forced to retreat over the Kuwaiti border and brace for the attack by coalition forces.

In late January, the coalition's focus shifted from strategic targets to preparing the battlefield for the ground war. Air attacks destroyed almost all of the Iraqi naval forces in the Persian Gulf. Other attacks destroyed Iraqi weapons on the

Hussein Survives

Hussein was never officially a target. Although it was not well publicized, coalition airmen felt at liberty to kill Hussein, who was believed to be hiding in a bunker northwest of Basra. On January 23, 1991, raids by U.S. warplanes failed in several strikes to hit Hussein. By the end of the war, coalition forces had launched an estimated 250 air raids aimed at Hussein with no success.

ground. Low-flying U.S. aircraft spotted Iraqi tanks and blew them up.

In the process, they dropped leaflets promising good treatment for Iraqi soldiers who surrendered. Some leaflets even warned of future attacks to promote panic and encourage surrender.

Hussein was not about to surrender, but many of his soldiers soon did just that. The Iraqis were demoralized by the relentless bombing and were quite aware that their control of Kuwait was not going to last much longer. ⌐

A U.S. jet fighter pilot signaled a successful mission over Iraq in January 1991.

On January 31, 1991, U.S. marines took cover from an Iraqi attack.

PLANNING THE
GROUND WAR

Saddam Hussein seemed less confident after the Instant Thunder air campaign began. He took to the airwaves on January 20, 1991, to flex his military muscle, though many believed his words were also intended to keep his courage up.

In his address to the people of Iraq, Hussein said,

In the coming period, the response of Iraq will be on a larger scale, using all means and potential God has given us and which we have so far only used in part. Our ground forces have not entered the battle so far. . . . The army's air force has not been used, nor has the navy. The weight of our missile force has not yet been applied in full.[1]

General Norman Schwarzkopf expressed his feelings to the coalition that their ground forces were ready. But he was concerned with the push-and-wait attack plan of the U.S. Army Seven (VII) Corps. He felt this type of attack was too slow for success. "I want VII Corps to 'slam' into the Republican Guard. . . . Go after them with audacity, shock action, and surprise."[2]

More than one-half million U.S. troops assembled to liberate Kuwait. To avoid more bloodshed, President Bush called for the Iraqi people to rise up and topple Hussein. That was not about to happen. The Iraqis would have to be forcibly removed from Kuwait.

Protecting Kuwait

General Schwarzkopf rejected the initial plan of a landing of marines by boat to start the ground assault. He believed that such a tactic would result in too many deaths, as well as great destruction of Kuwaiti properties on the coast. Schwarzkopf and other military officials took great care to make certain that as little damage was done to Kuwait as possible throughout the war.

Schwarzkopf ordered the ship-based Marines to divert the Iraqis by tricking them into defending the coastal areas. Meanwhile, the U.S. Army took up positions inland.

On February 18, Soviet leader Mikhail Gorbachev met with Iraqi Foreign Minister Tariq Aziz in an attempt to work out a solution. A plan was drawn up in which Iraq would withdraw all its forces from Kuwait within six weeks and the regime of Hussein would remain intact. The meeting of Gorbachev and Aziz was a surprise to Bush, who immediately rejected the plan. He insisted that Iraq leave Kuwait within four days and rejected several other stipulations.

Aziz and the Soviet representatives emerged with another peace proposal on February 21. But the new plan did not comply with United Nations (UN) resolutions. These included the repayment to Kuwait for the damage done to that country and the freedom of Kuwaitis held captive in Iraq. Bush saw little sense in giving Hussein conditions for leaving Kuwait when he was all but defeated.

Soon the ground attack plan was ready. Bush gave his approval for a U.S.-led coalition force strike between February 21 and 24. In an attempt to determine Iraqi troop strength in the area and convince the Iraqis that the main attack would be launched from Wadi al-Batin, U.S. Army troops began maneuvers there. The Iraqis attacked and killed three U.S. soldiers.

On the evening of February 22, Joint Chiefs of Staff Chairman General Colin Powell recommended that Bush give Gorbachev the following message: "If you get them out by noon Saturday [February 23], Mr. Gorbachev, you get the Nobel [Peace] Prize. If you don't, we kick Hussein's [butt]."[3]

Gorbachev could not secure an Iraqi withdrawal. As a result, Powell's threat was about to be fulfilled.

PLAN OF ATTACK

The ground war plan featured three areas of attack in what was known as the Kuwaiti Theater of Operations (KTO). These included Kuwait City, southern Iraq at the Saudi-Iraqi border, and a pathway between Basra and Baghdad.

Hussein's Revenge

Hussein understood defeat was near. In a move caused by frustration and revenge, the Iraqi dictator ordered Kuwaiti oil fields to be set on fire. Satellite images showed that in the month of February, approximately 700 out of nearly 1,000 oil wells experienced fires or other damage. The flames burned for months. If Hussein's country could not lay claim to the oil, he made certain that it would go to waste.

Troops from coalition forces spoke with awe about the number of troops involved in the launching of the ground war on February 24, 1991. They also had a difficult time soaking in the many attack plans. "I can't fathom the size of this operation," said U.S. pilot Lieutenant Colonel Randy Bigum. "I can't grasp it. It's enormous."[4]

The U.S. Marines joined forces with troops from Arab nations such as Saudi Arabia, Syria, and Egypt. The forces then moved from Saudi Arabia into Kuwait to recapture Kuwait City.

The U.S. Army Seven and Eight Corps was delegated to strike southern Iraq from the Saudi border. It was believed that weaker troops in the area were shielding the strength of the Iraqi military—the Republican Guard.

A surprise attack was also planned. Troops headed north to establish an operating base for aircraft west of the main battles. The base assumed control of the pathway between Basra and Baghdad.

As 10:00 p.m. approached on February 23 in Washington DC, President Bush strode to the podium. The coalition forces had already begun its assault to liberate Kuwait. Bush addressed the nation:

> *The liberation of Kuwait has entered a final phase. . . . What we have seen is a redoubling of Saddam Hussein's efforts to*

destroy completely Kuwait and its people. . . . Tonight, as this coalition seeks to do that which is right and just, I ask only that all of you stop what you are doing and say a prayer for all the coalition forces, and especially for our men and women in uniform, who at this very moment are risking their lives for their country and all of us.[5]

A Two-pronged Attack

Shortly after the president addressed the nation, forces from the United States, Great Britain, France, Kuwait, Saudi Arabia, and six other Arab nations

Words of Wisdom

As news of the early success of the ground war began filtering in, President Bush attended a service at Saint John's Episcopal Church in Washington DC. Presidents Abraham Lincoln, Woodrow Wilson, and Lyndon Johnson had prayed there during the wars of their generations, and now Bush was doing the same.

Bush listened as Rector John C. Harper spoke about the conflict in Iraq. "Ever since the war in the Persian Gulf began in January, a hymn has been running through my mind," Harper told the congregation. "The hymn is a prayer for peace, and it begins, 'O God of love, O King of peace, make wars throughout the world to cease.'"[6]

Harper criticized the United States and other democratic nations for failing to lead by example in showing their enemies the greatness and benefits of freedom. As Bush listened, he received a note from Defense Secretary Dick Cheney that assured him that the ground war was going better than anticipated.

At the White House after the church service, Cheney provided the president with more details. The Allied forces suffered only four casualties. Schwarzkopf would continue his advance.

launched the ground war in a two-pronged attack. It
was February 24, 4:00 a.m. Gulf time. The marine
assault struck Iraqi strongholds just over Kuwait's
border. The Iraqis could not halt the advance toward
Kuwait City.

The Iraqis had set up a treacherous path that
included fields filled with explosive devices called
mines. They used barbed wire and dangerous traps
such as trenches filled with boiling oil. The marines
passed the two minefields into Al-Burqan's oil field.
Iraqis who had vowed never to surrender broke their
vows and surrendered in droves. Less than two hours
later, a marine division destroyed an entire Iraqi
tank corps.

That same morning, the offensive launched
by the U.S. Army Seven Corps through the desert
proved surprising to the Iraqis. The Iraqis barely
defended themselves on the drive north from Saudi
Arabia into their own country.

The coalition troops headed east and defeated
the Republican Guard. A group from the U.S. Army
Seven Corps proceeded nine miles (14 km) into
Iraq. The Second Armored Cavalry looped around
the Iraqis and advanced approximately 50 miles
(80 km) into Iraqi territory before darkness set in.

An Iraqi prisoner's papers were inspected on February 25, 1991, the second full day of the ground war.

FAST AND FURIOUS

In just one day, more than 5,000 Iraqi troops surrendered. Many of them hoisted white surrender flags before the coalition forces even fired a shot. Desertion was rampant, even among Iraqi officers. Some kissed the hands of their captors.

Saudi General Prince Khalid bin Sultan, who was in charge of the Arab forces, felt his men did not believe in their cause. Unlike those who questioned the training and ability of the Iraqi forces, he considered a lack of spirit as the reason why the Iraqi troops gave up so easily. He said,

> *I'm not underestimating the Iraqi soldiers' ability and professionalism in fighting. . . . As a matter of fact, they are good. But there is one thing they are lacking, that they don't believe in what they are fighting for right now.*[7]

Even General Schwarzkopf might have been surprised by the swiftness of the advance and the lack of resistance from the Iraqis. Although he spoke with great optimism after the first day of the ground war, he cautioned that there was a long road ahead for the coalition forces.

The general emphasized that the offensive was a coalition effort. Little did he know that the war was almost over. Most assumed the Iraqis would defend Kuwait City. But as events unfolded, it became more apparent that the Iraqis were almost finished despite Hussein's attempt to defy the world.

The Iraqis issued a statement, "The enemy attack has failed utterly, and the scoundrels of aggressors are crying for help and swimming in their own blood. Victory is sweet."[8]

The coalition soon discovered that victory was indeed sweet. ⌐

Al-Burqan's oil field in Kuwait was set on fire by the Iraqis.

By February 25, 1991, General Colin Powell, chairman of the U.S. Joint Chiefs of Staff, was making plans to end the war.

SENDING IRAQ BACK

Many Iraqis surrendered willingly to the coalition forces as the ground war began. Many held leaflets that U.S. planes had dropped. The leaflets instructed the Iraqis to remove the cartridges from their weapons and to hold their guns upside down with their hands raised above their heads when they approached their captors. The leaflets also promised the Iraqis that they would not die in captivity.

Saddam Hussein had quite another message for his soldiers in a radio address from Baghdad:

> *O' Iraqis, fight them with all the power you have and all struggle for everything and all the faith you have in a people that believes in God and in his dignity and his rights to choose and select and make its own decisions. Fight them, brave Iraqis!*[1]

Iraqi military leaders gave another message: fight or die. An estimated 70,000 Iraqi soldiers managed to surrender during the one-sided ground war. But others who tried to surrender were tortured and killed by Iraqi officers. Some were even beheaded for deserting.

Camp officials in Saudi Arabia were overwhelmed. They expected

Surrender

According to General Schwarzkopf, many Iraqis did not realize the ground war had begun until tanks rolled over their positions. The attack was moving so quickly that some coalition troops collected the weapons of surrendering Iraqis without even taking them prisoners. They simply pointed the Iraqis to the direction in which they were to surrender, then continued forward.

fewer than 1,000 prisoners on the first day of the ground war. In the first ten hours, more than 5,500 Iraqi prisoners had arrived. The promises printed in the leaflets were kept. The prisoners were fed and treated with far more respect than the Iraqis had shown to the Kuwaiti people they had attacked only six months earlier.

The main ground attack still waited at the Saudi border. A massive force of 1,600 heavy tanks represented the United States, Great Britain, and France. They were ready to meet three main objectives: free Kuwait City, destroy the Republican Guard, and block Iraqi escape routes.

The original plan was to wait until the second day of the ground war to send the tanks forward. The ground offensive was so far ahead of schedule that General Norman Schwarzkopf ordered the attack at 3:00 p.m. on the first day. After all, Iraqi resistance was collapsing.

The main thrust of the Desert Storm attack was a success. Less than two hours after it began, a French division, supported by U.S. paratroopers, was in the process of overrunning 10,000 Iraqi troops and capturing the town of As-Salman. Iraqi supply trucks were being destroyed by fire from Apache helicopters

along the main road. The 24th
Mechanized Division had rumbled
35 miles (56 km) into Iraq.

By the end of the evening,
Schwarzkopf called Lieutenant
General Walt Boomer to congratulate
him on the first-day success of the
ground war. Schwarzkopf was quite
satisfied, but also wary of what was to
come the next day. He still believed
a strong Iraqi counterattack was
forthcoming.

The 24th Mechanized Infantry
Division did not slow down at
nightfall. By morning it had pushed
approximately 60 miles (97 km)
into Iraq, but the U.S. Army Seven Corps had been
slowed a bit. They still had not struck the Republican
Guard. At this point, only eight U.S. soldiers had
been killed and 27 wounded, which greatly relieved
General Schwarzkopf.

Just about Over

By the end of February 25, General Colin
Powell was already making plans to end the war.

Second Day Losses

The U.S. troops did not go
unharmed on the second
day of the ground war.
An Iraqi Scud missile ex-
ploded in Dhahran, Saudi
Arabia, killing 28 and
wounding 99 U.S. Army
Reserve troops, according
to the U.S. Department of
Defense. Patriot missiles
tracking the Scud were
too far away to fire at it.
Meanwhile, faulty track-
ing equipment failed to
detect the missile, which
exploded at a warehouse
where the U.S. soldiers
were staying.

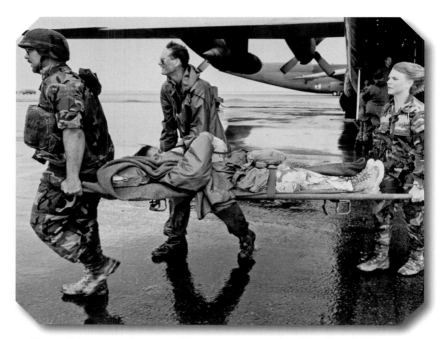

Desert Storm casualty carried by U.S. Army medics on February 25, 1991

He informed General Schwarzkopf that a speedy conclusion seemed fairly certain. He explained to President Bush that "it's not going to be long" since the coalition troops were "close to breaking the Iraqi Army." He later added that "this is over; all we're doing is killing people."[2]

The coalition forces were now preparing their final thrust to remove the Iraqis from Kuwait. The Iraqis had stepped up their resistance, particularly on the coast, where marines had fought off three

Iraqi counterattacks. In the process, many Iraqi tanks were destroyed and one marine had been killed. Meanwhile, troops from the Arab nations easily marched along and were given the go-ahead to attempt to reach Kuwait City.

The major Iraqi offensive from Republican Guard troops that coalition force commanders expected simply never occurred. Republican Guardsmen retreated from their defensive positions. The U.S. Army Seven Corps headed east to attack the Republican Guard forces. This played a major role in the quick defeat of the Iraqi military.

So did the march north by the 24th Mechanized Infantry Division, which traveled approximately 150 miles (240 km) in a 24-hour period. This was faster than any ground force had traveled in the history of warfare. The division moved east toward Basra to cut off Republican Guard forces trying to escape the U.S. Army Seven Corps. British troops also marched east to destroy another Iraqi tank division and reach Kuwait.

Soon, what was left of the Republican Guard was trapped outside of Basra. The U.S. 101st Airborne Division had cut off any fresh troops or supplies from reaching them. The only concerted efforts by Iraqi forces occurred in southern Kuwait. The marines won tank battles near the Burqan oil fields before moving on to take control of the Kuwait International Airport and the Kuwait City suburb of Al-Jahrah.

Late on the night of February 25, and continuing for the next two days, Iraqi troops, tanks, and other motorized vehicles fled Kuwait City on Highway 6. They were attacked and destroyed by U.S. warplanes, whose pilots had an easy time finding their targets. Many of the Iraqis fled to the desert with money and other valuables stolen from Kuwaiti homes.

A Military Destroyed

There are no exact statistics of the devastation the Iraqi military experienced by the co-alition forces. However, the constant bombing and eventual ground war destroyed Hussein's hope of making Iraq a major world power or a dominant state in the Arab world.

The Iraqi Air Force, which entered the war as the sixth largest in the world, was severely damaged. Its combat aircraft fleet was reduced from approximately 750 to 324. Its navy was never strong, but now it was completely destroyed in the war.

Most of Iraq's tanks were outdated Russian tanks. The Republican Guard had a few advanced T-72 tanks, but even these were no match for the U.S. M1 Abrams or British Challenger tanks. Iraqi tanks had been cut from 5,800 to an estimated 3,200.

Hussein's ability to develop nuclear weapons was also greatly affected. After the Gulf War, United Nations (UN) inspectors discovered that Iraq had been within two years of realizing that goal, but consistent air attacks ruined its nuclear capabilities. Desert Storm and UN inspection teams made certain that Hussein could not revitalize his nuclear weapon production for quite a while.

"I could see Iraqi trucks from a long distance," said one U.S. pilot about what became known as the Highway of Death. "I then locked on target and fired away knowing that the hapless Iraqi on the other end never had a chance."[3]

The idea of U.S. fighters picking off helpless Iraqis when the war had been all but won did not sit well with the president. He feared an unpleasant reaction from the media and U.S. citizens. That helped Bush decide to call for a cease-fire, but not until the Iraqi military was defeated.

Who Won?

The following day, Hussein announced on Baghdad Radio that his troops were pulling out of Kuwait. It was apparent from his speech that he learned little from the experience and blamed the United States and its allies for the conflict. After announcing that he was withdrawing from Kuwait, he actually claimed Iraq had won the war, at least from a moral standpoint.

> *Today certain circumstances made the Iraqi Army withdraw . . . including the combined aggression by 30 countries. . . . The soldiers of faith have triumphed over the*

soldiers of wrong, O stalwart men. Your God is the one who granted your victory. You triumphed when you rejected, in the name of faith, the will of evil which the evildoers wanted to impose on you to kill the fire of faith in your hearts. . . . Victory is sweet with the help of God.[4]

President Bush did not believe for a moment that Hussein had ordered the withdrawal of his troops. The president said, "He is not withdrawing. His defeated forces are retreating. . . . The forces will therefore continue . . . the war with undiminished intensity."[5]

Despite Hussein's claim of withdrawal, the coalition strategy remained the same on February 26 as it had been six weeks earlier: force Iraq out of Kuwait until that country was free again.

Soon that goal would become a reality. ⸺

U.S. Marines guarded hundreds of Iraqi prisoners
as they marched toward the Saudi border.

General Schwarzkopf pointed to the position of troops during a February 27, 1991, press briefing.

KUWAIT IS FREE AGAIN

While Saddam Hussein trumpeted a moral triumph in the Gulf War, there were doubts that he had withdrawn his troops from Kuwait—and rightly so. There was to be more fighting, at least on February 26.

On the final day of the 100-hour ground war, coalition forces destroyed 22 Iraqi divisions. The Republican Guard was not withdrawing. It sent tanks and soldiers against the U.S. Second Cavalry Regiment in the Battle of 73 Easting. The fiercely fought six-hour battle marked one of the few Iraqi offensives of the war. However, the Republican Guard lost 90 tanks in this battle compared to the loss of one U.S. Bradley.

Just as every Iraqi offensive in the Gulf War, this one proved futile. Meanwhile, the French were finishing off Iraqi resistance at the As-Salman airfield.

The Iraqis were unsuccessful in Kuwait and surrendered in large numbers. Marines took in willing prisoners as they continued on to liberate Kuwait City. The Kuwait International Airport was seized by coalition troops early on February 27. The marines captured the Kuwait City suburb of Al-Jahrah despite a fight from Iraqi soldiers.

Kuwait was anxious for the Iraqis to lose their grip on Kuwait City. A victorious tank battle allowed 12 marines to become the first coalition troops to enter Kuwait's capital. The American embassy was taken back by the evening of February 26.

Further fighting occurred on February 27. This included a one-sided tank battle against Republican Guardsmen. In essence, the war was over. President Bush smiled as he announced that Kuwait was once again free:

> *Iraq's Army is defeated. Our military objectives are met. Kuwait is once more in the hands of Kuwaitis in control of their own destiny. The Kuwaiti flag once again flies above the capital of a free and sovereign nation, and the American flag flies above our embassy.*[1]

It took nearly seven months after Iraq's invasion of Kuwait to comply, but on March 1, Iraq officially agreed to accept the United Nations (UN) Security Council resolution calling for withdrawal.

However, on March 1 and 2, the U.S. Army's 24th Mechanized Infantry Division was attacked by two Republican Guard battalions. This led to several hours of fighting. Nearly 200 Iraqi tanks, 11 missile systems, and 23 trucks were destroyed. An additional 3,000 Iraqi soldiers were taken prisoner.

ALL OVER BUT THE SIGNING

On March 3, Iraqi generals met with General Norman Schwarzkopf and other coalition military leaders in a tent at Safwan airfield to sign the cease-fire agreement. Though Bush declared the war over a week earlier, the Iraqi military finally surrendered on March 3.

The Iraqi Army was indeed defeated, yet Hussein was still the country's dictator. President Bush hoped the destructive war would motivate Iraqis to rid themselves of Hussein. And, in fact, a great deal of civil unrest did occur shortly after the cease-fire. Kurds drove Hussein's forces out of Kurdistan in northern Iraq while fighting also spread

Cease-fire!

The top priority for military officials when discussing a cease-fire with Iraq was the release of all coalition prisoners of war. There was a good reason for that. It took decades to account for many of the prisoners of war and those missing in action during the Vietnam War. The fate of some others still has not been determined. U.S. military officials did not want a repeat of such agony for the families of soldiers who were not yet identified.

Another concern was making the former battlefields safe for coalition troops leaving the area. General Schwarzkopf made certain that the Iraqis pointed out every spot on land and sea where they had placed exploding mines and other booby traps in Kuwait.

Finally, it was determined that the Iraqi military and coalition forces must be separated as they left the theater of war. Any contact between the two, even after the cease-fire was concluded, could result in fighting and needless loss of life.

Colin Powell and General Schwarzkopf made certain all those points were placed into the cease-fire agreement before it was signed. The signing of the cease-fire marked the first time that both Iraqi and coalition military personnel spoke face-to-face.

A U.S. Special Forces soldier was surrounded by Kuwaitis on February 27, 1991, when Kuwait City was liberated from Iraq.

from Basra to cities such as An Nasiriya and Karbala. A Shiite uprising against Hussein's regime was also reported in southeast Iraq.

Hussein reacted to the rebellions with brutality and ordered his Republican Guard into Shiite neighborhoods to slaughter citizens. He publicly hanged many as a lesson to others not to fight against his rule. He then turned his attention to the Kurdish rebels and called for attacks that killed thousands of men, women, and children. By early

April, all resistance against Hussein's regime had ended.

After the war, the Iraqi dictator proved to be as ruthless as ever. His actions made many question if the fight should have continued until Hussein was removed from power or at least his military capabilities were eliminated. Even though the war had destroyed much of their weaponry, the Iraqis had been allowed to escape with a great deal of it still intact. Hussein reported in mid-April that he still had 10,000 nerve-gas warheads, 1,000 tons (907 tonnes) of mustard and nerve gas, 1,500 chemical weapons, and 30 Scud missiles in his arsenal.

Refugees

The brutal aggression by Hussein's henchmen against Kurdish rebels sent many Kurds streaming from Iraq into neighboring Turkey. Coalition troops and humanitarian groups helped by providing food, shelter, clothing, and medical care to the refugees.

Schwarzkopf seemed to change his mind on that subject.

> *I think I've made it clear to everybody that I'd just as soon the war had never started, and I'd just as soon never have lost a single life out there. That was not our choice. We've accomplished our mission, and when the decision-makers come to the decision that there should be a cease-fire, nobody will be happier than me.*[2]

One month later, however, Schwarzkopf expressed to interviewer David Frost that "my recommendation had been to continue to march" because President Bush's decision to end the war "did leave some escape routes open for [the Iraqis] to get back out."[3]

Joy and Criticism

Perhaps the issue was lost in the joy of postwar celebrations. Schwarzkopf returned from Iraq to a hero's welcome. He was cheered in parades in Washington DC, New York, and other cities. U.S. troops were greeted by the open arms of a grateful public. This was a stunning contrast to how U.S. troops were ignored or ridiculed when they returned from the unpopular Vietnam War in the late 1960s and early 1970s.

But as time elapsed, it became apparent that Hussein continued to be a vicious dictator. His continued brutality against his people motivated many to regret the decision against working toward his removal from power. Although he did not start more conflicts against other nations, some believed it was the moral obligation of the United States to help the Iraqis rid themselves of Hussein.

Schwarzkopf had a ready answer for those critics. He knew that ending Hussein's power in Iraq would have required fighting all the way to Baghdad. He also recognized this would have resulted in the loss of thousands of lives. In his autobiography, he wrote:

> *It should be understood that the option of going all the way to Baghdad was never considered. . . . There was not a single head of state, diplomat, Middle East expert or military leader who, as far as I am aware, advocated continuing the war and seizing Baghdad.*
>
> *The United Nations resolutions that provided the legal basis for our military operations in the gulf were clear in their intent: kick the Iraqi military force out of Kuwait. We had authority to take whatever actions were necessary to accomplish that mission, including attacks into Iraq. But we had no authority to invade Iraq for the purpose of capturing the entire country or its capital.*[4]

And though Hussein remained in power, the world had changed as a result of the Gulf War. It was proven that the UN worked in times of crisis. Nations from around the world, including Iraq's Arab neighbors, had banded together to right an injustice. And the United States was able to convince Israel not to respond when attacked. This single

A City under Siege

Baghdad was barely recognizable after the war. The Iraqi capital had developed into one of the most modern cities in the Middle East, but now it had no heat, no electricity, no working telephones or traffic lights, no postal service, and no working toilets for its 4 million people. Even the skyline had changed. Because of poor medical conditions, diseases ran rampant.

achievement may have prevented war from spreading throughout the Middle East.

Such efforts were critical to the United States. The nation had regained confidence in its military and government during times of crisis. But as events unfolded, the decision by Bush to refrain from ousting Hussein would be questioned.

Bush's son, future president George W. Bush, would attempt to take on that responsibility under even more criticism a decade later.

An Operation Welcome Home parade in New York City on June 10, 1991

World Trade Center after the September 11, 2001, attacks

WHAT HAVE WE
LEARNED?

On the morning of September 11, 2001, terrorists hijacked U.S. passenger planes and flew them directly into the two World Trade Center skyscrapers in New York City. Thousands of innocent people were killed.

That same day, two more hijacked planes crashed. One hit the Pentagon, which is the military center of the United States. The heroism of the passengers on the other plane forced the plane down in Pennsylvania before it reached its target. But in both cases, hundreds more lost their lives.

Taking credit for the hijackings and the killing of thousands was al-Qaeda, a terrorist organization based in the Middle East and led by Osama bin Laden. Terrorists use threats and violent action in an attempt to achieve their goals.

Al-Qaeda

Osama bin Laden is credited with founding al-Qaeda, which is made up of terrorist cells worldwide. Both the United Nations Security Council and the U.S. State Department label al-Qaeda as a terrorist organization. The goals of al-Qaeda include forcing any U.S. presence out of Saudi Arabia and any Muslim nation, as well as overthrowing non-Islamic governments.

President George W. Bush, whose father was president and directed U.S. efforts during the Gulf War, claimed that Saddam Hussein cooperated with the terrorists in planning the actions of September 11. President Bush was also certain that Iraq was producing weapons of mass destruction (WMD) such as chemical, biological, and nuclear weapons. Hussein denied it and eventually gave United Nations (UN) weapons inspectors access to his facilities.

Meanwhile, Bush received the backing he needed from Congress to wage war. On March 19, 2003, he announced that the conflict he called Operation Iraqi Freedom had begun. In a speech to the nation, Bush stated:

> *The people of the United States and our friends and allies will not live at the mercy of an outlaw regime that threatens the peace with weapons of mass murder. We will meet that threat now, with our Army, Air Force, Navy, Coast Guard and Marines. . . .*
>
> *Now that the conflict has come, the only way to limit its duration is to apply decisive force. And I assure you, this will not be a campaign of half measures, and we will accept no outcome but victory.*
>
> *My fellow citizens, the dangers to our country and the world will be overcome. We will pass through this time of peril and carry on the work of peace. We will defend our freedom. We will bring freedom to others and we will prevail.*[1]

Initially, seven nations joined in the effort led by the United States that started the following day. Though the coalition troops had to fight through some resistance, they easily entered Baghdad and overthrew Hussein's regime.

WRONG REASONS FOR WAR?

At about the time that Hussein fled, the UN inspectors revealed that they had found no traces of weapons of mass destruction in Iraq. Many who had been against the war from the beginning stepped up their protests. Members of Congress, including many who had voted for the war, changed their opinions and claimed Bush had led the nation to battle under false pretenses.

Hussein eventually was captured. But Bush became increasingly unpopular in the United States as radicals and terrorists from various religious

Weapons of Mass Destruction

The United States dropped the first atomic bomb on Hiroshima, Japan, to end World War II in 1945. Since that moment, world leaders have worked to keep weapons of mass destruction out of the hands of those considered dangerous enough to use them.

Among those thought of as dangerous was Iraqi dictator Saddam Hussein. Some reports indicated that Hussein was gathering the materials to manufacture nuclear weapons.

In March 2003, inspectors from the United Nations searched for evidence that Iraq was actively building weapons of mass destruction, but found none. Bush decided to carry out his threat against Hussein as the United States launched Operation Iraqi Freedom two days after the inspectors left the country.

Since that time, however, it has been determined that while Hussein might have been seeking nuclear capabilities years ago, the program had been halted well before 2003. Many leaders and others in the United States and around the world have condemned the invasion on what they believe to be false pretenses.

groups in Iraq brought that nation to the brink of civil war. Hundreds of Iraqis were murdered every week by terrorist acts as U.S. troops tried to keep peace. Meanwhile, the number of U.S. deaths continued to increase to over 4,000 in early 2008. And bin Laden had yet to be captured or killed.

Perhaps the most notable differences between the Gulf War and Operation Iraqi Freedom are the missions themselves and world support. During the Gulf War crisis, the United States and coalition forces fought to right a wrong. Iraq had ruthlessly attacked and conquered Kuwait. It was universally accepted that such a takeover could not be tolerated.

Such a clear-cut moral reason for attacking Iraq in 2003 was missing, particularly after U.S. inspectors found no weapons of mass destruction. It also was not established that Hussein had any role in the terrorist attacks of 2001. Yet Bush had stated those two factors as reasons for launching the war in 2003. By 2004, some looked upon the United States as an occupying force in Iraq.

After Hussein was forced out of power, Bush stated an objective of making Iraq a democratic country that would be a beacon of freedom for the Middle East. Many did not believe such a goal was realistic. Some who felt it was attainable did not think it was worth waiting for as the death toll of U.S. soldiers and Iraqi citizens continued to increase.

RIGHT VERSUS WRONG

Few in the United States, or in most nations around the world, have doubted that Hussein was a brutal tyrant. The vast majority approved his removal from power.

But U.S. citizens and others asked if the United States had the moral authority to act as the world's police force. Many question whether the United States has the right to remove world leaders by force even if those leaders pose no immediate danger.

When no weapons of mass destruction were found, the threat of Hussein was questioned. Yet, U.S. troops remained in Iraq even though most U.S. citizens believed they should be sent home. Bush claimed that the United States was acting in self-defense when Operation Iraqi Freedom began. The realization that Iraq did not boast weapons of mass destruction and the contention that Hussein had no role in the terrorist attacks in 2001 led many to question whether or not the United States was indeed acting in self-defense.

During the Gulf War, world leaders and U.S. citizens believed what the U.S. government was doing to rid Kuwait of Hussein was right. Those same world leaders and most U.S. citizens followed Bush and Operation Iraqi Freedom for a while, but many strayed when they no longer believed the mission in Iraq was justified.

In the Gulf War, most believed that the soldiers who were killed died for a just cause. Four years after Operation Iraqi Freedom, Iraq was free of Hussein, but not free of terror. Everyone has a different concept about right and wrong. But in the Gulf War, the world virtually agreed: U.S. troops and others fought for what was right. ⌒

On November 3, 2004, National Guard troops waited to leave for training at Fort Lewis, Washington, before deployment to Iraq.

TIMELINE

1979	1980	1990
Saddam Hussein becomes president of Iraq on July 16. He begins a campaign against all perceived enemies.	Iraq declares war against Iran on September 4 and invades that country on September 22.	On July 16, Hussein accuses Kuwait of stealing $2.4 billion in oil from a field Iraq claims to own.

1990	1990	1990
The League of Arab States votes on August 3 to condemn the attack.	The United States sends warships to the Persian Gulf and the Red Sea to defend Saudi Arabia on August 7.	Congress votes on October 1–2 to support President Bush in regard to Iraq.

1990	1990	1990
On July 17, Iraq threatens war against Kuwait and the United Arab Emirates for driving down the price of oil.	On July 26, Iraq masses troops on the Kuwaiti border. Kuwait reinstates its military alert.	Iraq invades Kuwait on August 2. The UN Security Council condemns the invasion.

1990	1990	1991
Bush orders more troops to the Persian Gulf region on November 8. Schwarzkopf prepares for Desert Storm.	On November 29, the UN Security Council calls for war if Iraq does not leave Kuwait by midnight, January 15, 1991.	At 6:38 p.m. EST on January 16, the White House announces that the liberation of Kuwait has begun.

TIMELINE

1991	1991	1991
Iraq launches its first Scud missiles toward Israel and Saudi Arabia on January 18.	The coalition ground assault against Iraq in Kuwait and Iraq begins on February 24.	Coalition forces advance in Kuwait and Iraq on February 25.

1991	1991	1991
U.S. troops begin returning home in March.	The war officially ends on April 11.	A victory parade is held on June 8.

1991

1991

1991

Hussein announces a withdrawal from Kuwait and claims a moral victory on February 26.

On February 27, Bush announces Kuwait has been liberated.

Coalition military leaders meet with Iraqi generals on March 3 to discuss the cease-fire.

2001

2003

2003

Planes hijacked by terrorists fly into the World Trade Center and two other sites on September 11.

The United States and coalition forces begin a new war against Iraq on March 20.

Hussein's government is forced out of power in Iraq on April 9.

Essential Facts

Date of Event

August 2, 1990, to February 27, 1991

Place of Event

Iraq, Kuwait, Saudi Arabia

Key Players

- ❖ Iraqi President Saddam Hussein
- ❖ U.S. President George H. W. Bush
- ❖ General Norman Schwarzkopf
- ❖ U.S. and coalition forces
- ❖ Iraqi Republican Guard forces

Highlights of Event

- ❖ Hussein ordered an attack on Kuwait on August 2, 1990.
- ❖ U.S. and coalition troops moved into the Middle East throughout the summer of 1990 as Operation Desert Shield began.
- ❖ United Nations Security Council and Arab League countries voted to condemn the invasion of Kuwait and order Iraq to withdraw from Kuwait.
- ❖ Peace talks with the Soviet Union and the United States failed as the January 15, 1991, deadline for Iraq to pull out of Kuwait neared.
- ❖ Operation Desert Storm began on January 16, 1991, as coalition warplanes destroyed military and communications centers in the Iraqi capital of Baghdad.

❖ Coalition troops moved easily through Iraq and Kuwait during the 100-hour ground war that began on February 24, 1991.

❖ Hussein announced a withdrawal from Kuwait and a moral victory in the war on February 26, 1991. Coalition forces remained on their missions as Iraqi troops continued resistance.

❖ The Iraqis signed a cease-fire on March 3, 1991. Hussein remained in power and sent troops to quell Kurdish and Shiite rebellions in his country.

QUOTE

"Our objectives are clear: Saddam Hussein's forces will leave Kuwait. The legitimate government of Kuwait will be restored to its rightful place, and Kuwait will once again be free. Iraq will eventually comply with all relevant United Nations resolutions, and then, when peace is restored, it is our hope that Iraq will live as a peaceful and cooperative member of the family of nations, thus enhancing the security and stability of the Gulf." —*President George H. W. Bush, in a speech announcing the war against Iraq, January 16, 1991*

ADDITIONAL RESOURCES

SELECT BIBLIOGRAPHY

Allen, Thomas B., F. Clifton Berry, and Norman Polmar. *War in the Gulf*. Atlanta, GA: Turner Publishing, Inc., 1991.

Atkinson, Rick. *Crusade: The Untold Story of the Persian Gulf War*. Boston: Houghton Mifflin Company, 1993.

Gordon, Michael R., and Bernard E. Trainor. *The Generals' War*. Boston: Little, Brown and Company, 1995.

Palmer, Michael A. *Guardians of the Gulf*. New York: The Free Press, 1992.

Schwartz, Richard Alan. *Encyclopedia of the Persian Gulf War*. Jefferson, NC: McFarland & Company, Inc., 1998.

Schwarzkopf, Norman H., and Peter Petre. *It Doesn't Take a Hero*. New York: Bantam Books, 1992.

Sciolino, Elaine. *The Outlaw State*. New York: John Wiley & Sons, 1991.

Yetiv, Steve A. *The Persian Gulf Crisis*. Westport, CT: Greenwood Press, 1997.

FURTHER READING

Deegan, Paul. *Operation Desert Storm (War in the Gulf)*. Edina, MN: ABDO Publishing Company, 1991.

Gay, Kathlyn, and Martin K. Gay. *Persian Gulf Wars*. New York: 21st Century Books, 1996.

Miller, Mary. *The Brave Women of the Gulf War: Operation Desert Storm and Operation Iraqi Freedom*. New York: 21st Century Books, 2006.

Web Links

To learn more about Operation Desert Storm, visit ABDO Publishing Company online at **www.abdopublishing.com**. Web sites about Operation Desert Storm are featured on our Book Links page. These links are routinely monitored and updated to provide the most current information available.

Places to Visit

Arlington National Cemetery
Memorial Bridge Drive, Arlington, VA 22211
703-607-8000
www.arlingtoncemetery.org/index.htm
Visit the Gulf War Memorial Stone at the Arlington National Cemetery. Pay tribute to the 25 soldiers buried there who were killed in the Gulf War.

George Bush Presidential Library and Museum
1000 George Bush Drive West, College Station, TX 77845
979-691-4000
http://bushlibrary.tamu.edu
Visit the Gulf War exhibit. Interactive displays and maps detail the battles. A program in the tent theater includes stories from military personnel who experienced the action.

Mississippi Armed Forces Museum
The Gulf War Gallery
Training Site, Building 850, Camp Shelby, MS 39407
601-558-2757
http://armedforcesmuseum.us/
Exhibits feature weapons and equipment of the Gulf War (Operations Desert Shield and Desert Storm), a miniature diorama of air and ground force coordination, and a life-sized diorama of Iraqis surrendering to U.S. forces.

GLOSSARY

artillery
  Mounted guns that fire missiles and other weapons.

assault
  To attack aggressively.

cease-fire
  An agreement by countries at war to stop fighting.

coalition
  A group of countries fighting for a common cause.

embargo
  The act of a nation to refuse to send goods or services to a particular country or countries as a means of protest.

extremist
  Radical thoughts or actions, particularly in political matters.

fundamentalist
  An individual who follows strict religious guidelines in his or her actions and lifestyle.

general
  The highest-ranking official in the U.S. Army, Air Force, or Marine Corps.

hostage
  A person held captive against his or her will.

independence
  The act of a country receiving or gaining freedom from control by another country.

liberation
  Freeing a country held captive against its will.

missile
  A weapon used during war that is launched against specific targets.

morality
  The subjective question of what is right and wrong.

Muslim
> A follower of the Islamic faith.

negotiations
> The act of reaching an agreement.

offensive
> An attack by one side against the other in time of war.

prophet
> A person who teaches a religious belief to others.

quell
> To forcefully put a stop to a certain act or behavior.

radar
> An electronic device that detects the presence and location of an object such as a missile during wartime.

rebellion
> Open resistance or violence against a government or a ruler.

resolution
> A formal expression of intent made by a group.

terrorism
> The use of violence or threats in an attempt to attain political goals.

United Nations
> An international organization based in New York City that promotes peace and security throughout the world.

U.S. Defense Secretary
> The person who is responsible for making military decisions for the United States.

withdraw
> To pull out willingly or by force during wartime.

SOURCE NOTES

Chapter 1. Fire from the Sky

1. Elaine Sciolino. *The Outlaw State*. New York: John Wiley & Sons, 1991. 244.
2. Michael R. Gordon and General Bernard E. Trainor. *The Generals' War*. Boston: Little, Brown and Company, 1995. 213.
3. Thomas B. Allen, F. Clifton Berry, and Norman Polmar. *War in the Gulf*. Atlanta, GA: Turner Publishing, Inc., 1991. 124.
4. Encyclopedia Britannica Profiles The American Presidency. "George Bush: Operation Desert Storm." 29 Feb. 2008 <http://www.britannica.com/presidents/article-9398251>.
5. Thomas B. Allen, F. Clifton Berry, and Norman Polmar. *War in the Gulf*. Atlanta, GA: Turner Publishing, Inc., 1991. 126.

Chapter 2. Seeds of Discontent

1. Michael A. Palmer. *Guardians of the Gulf*. New York: The Free Press, 1992. 214.
2. Ibid. 42.

Chapter 3. Collision Course

1. Elaine Sciolino. *The Outlaw State*. New York: John Wiley & Sons, 1991. 107.
2. Steve A. Yetiv. *The Persian Gulf Crisis*. Westport, CT: Greenwood Press, 1997. 5.
3. Elaine Sciolino. *The Outlaw State*. New York: John Wiley & Sons, 1991. 115.
4. Ibid. 112.
5. Ibid. 166.

Chapter 4. Killing in Kuwait

1. Lisa Beyer. "Iraq's Power Grab." *Time* 13 Aug. 1990: 16.
2. Thomas B. Allen, F. Clifton Berry, and Norman Polmar. *War in the Gulf*. Atlanta, GA: Turner Publishing, Inc., 1991. 72.
3. Lisa Beyer. "Iraq's Power Grab." *Time* 13 Aug. 1990: 16.
4. Bruce Nelan. "Call to arms: Bush issues his sternest warning yet to Saddam, and despite Tehran's call for a holy war against the U.S., the coalition against Iraq grows stronger." *Time* 24 Sept. 1990: 32.

5. Michael A. Palmer. *Guardians of the Gulf*. New York: The Free Press, 1992. 190.

Chapter 5. First Phase of War
1. H. Norman Schwarzkopf and Peter Petre. *It Doesn't Take a Hero*. New York: Bantam Books, 1992. 413.
2. Elaine Sciolino. *The Outlaw State*. New York: John Wiley & Sons, 1991. 255.
3. Michael R. Gordon and General Bernard E. Trainor. *The Generals' War*. Boston: Little, Brown and Company, 1995. 288.

Chapter 6. Planning the Ground War
1. Michael A. Palmer. *Guardians of the Gulf*. New York: The Free Press, 1992. 222.
2. H. Norman Schwarzkopf and Peter Petre. *It Doesn't Take a Hero*. New York: Bantam Books, 1992. 433.
3. Richard Alan Schwartz. *Encyclopedia of the Persian Gulf War*. Jefferson, NC: McFarland & Company, Inc., 1998. 60.
4. R.W. Apple Jr. "A War in the Gulf: The Overview; Allies Report Fast Advances in Iraq and Kuwait, With Little Resistance; Thousands of Iraqis Taken Prisoner." *New York Times*. 25 Feb. 1991. 4 Apr. 2008 <http://query.nytimes.com/gst/fullpage.html?res=9D0CE2D7143FF934A15751C0A967958260&sec=&spon=&pagewanted=4>.
5. Rick Atkinson. *Crusade: The Untold Story of the Persian Gulf War*. Boston: Houghton Mifflin Company, 1993. 376.
6. Ibid. 398.
7. Elaine Sciolino. *The Outlaw State*. New York: John Wiley & Sons, 1991. 259.
8. R.W. Apple Jr. "A War in the Gulf: The Overview; Allies Report Fast Advances in Iraq and Kuwait, With Little Resistance; Thousands of Iraqis Taken Prisoner." *New York Times*, 25 Feb. 1991. 4 Apr. 2008 <http://query.nytimes.com/gst/fullpage.html?res=9D0CE2D7143FF934A15751C0A967958260&sec=&spon=&pagewanted=4>.

Source Notes Continued

Chapter 7. Sending Iraq Back

1. Thomas B. Allen, F. Clifton Berry, and Norman Polmar. *War in the Gulf*. Atlanta, GA: Turner Publishing, Inc., 1991. 203.

2. Rick Atkinson. *Crusade: The Untold Story of the Persian Gulf War*. Boston: Houghton Mifflin Company, 1993. 449.

3. Steve A. Yetiv. *The Persian Gulf Crisis*. Westport, CT: Greenwood Press, 1997. 41.

4. "War in the Gulf: The Iraqi Leader; Saddam Hussein's Speech on the 'Withdrawal' of His Army from Kuwait." *New York Times* 27 Feb. 1991.

5. Richard Alan Schwartz. *Encyclopedia of the Persian Gulf War*. Jefferson, NC: McFarland & Company, Inc., 1998. 200.

Chapter 8. Kuwait Is Free Again

1. Andrew Rosenthal. "Military Aims Met: Firing Ending After 100 Hours of Ground War, President Declares." *New York Times* 28 Feb. 1991: A1.

2. Michael A. Palmer. *Guardians of the Gulf*. New York: The Free Press, 1992. 239.

3. Ibid.

4. H. Norman Schwarzkopf and Peter Petre. *It Doesn't Take a Hero*. New York: Bantam Books, 1992. 497.

Chapter 9. What Have We Learned?

1. George W. Bush. "President Bush Addresses the Nation." Speech delivered 19 Mar. 2003. 24 Oct. 2007 <http://www.state.gov/p/nea/rls/rm/18851.htm>.

2. George W. Bush. The White House Interview of the President by Pentagon Channel/AFN 19 Mar. 2008. 24 Mar. 2008 <http://www.whitehouse.gov/news/releases/2008/03/20080319-16.html>.

INDEX

Index Continued

ABOUT THE AUTHOR

Martin Gitlin was a reporter for two newspapers in northeast Ohio for 20 years before becoming solely a freelance writer. During his two decades as a reporter, Gitlin won more than 40 awards, including first place for general excellence from the Associated Press (AP) in 1995. AP also named him one of the top four features writers in the state of Ohio in 2001. Gitlin has written several educational books about sports and history.

PHOTO CREDITS

Sadayuki Mikami/AP Images, cover, 45; John McCutcheon/AP Images, 6; David Ake/Getty Images, 13; Dennis Cook/AP Images, 14; AP Images, 19, 24, 28, 52, 68; Time & Life Pictures/Getty Images, 23; Allan Tannenbaum/Time & Life Pictures/Getty Images, 33; Marty Lederhandler/AP Images, 34; Greg English/AP Images, 41; Peter Dejong/AP Images, 46, 58, 67; Martin Cleaver/AP Images, 51; Mark Peters/Time & Life Pictures/Getty Images, 57; Laurent Rebours/AP Images, 65, 82; Dennis Brack/Time & Life Pictures/Getty Images, 72; Tony O'Brien/Time & Life Pictures/Getty Images, 77; Greg Gibson/AP Images, 78; Susan Ragan/AP Images, 87; Alex Fuchs/AFP/Getty Images, 88; Michael Smith/AP Images, 95